"If you've never created anything, but spend time
criticising the work of others, you're a prick."

Mother Teresa, 2014

Your content's probably shit.

Don't panic. You're not alone.

Most people, and companies for that matter, produce content that's about as effective as a crepe paper condom.

Don't believe me?

Take a look at the social accounts of brands. At company blogs. At promoted content that appears on your feeds.

I guarantee the majority of the stuff you look at will have very little engagement, and from the engagement the content did get, very little of it comes from that company's ideal customer.

Why?

Because it's probably one of two things (or often both).

It's either more boring than bird watching with Bill Oddy, or it's trying to sell something. And nobody wants to be sold to.

So how do you make sure your content stands out? How do you use your social accounts, blogs and eBooks to drive new customers?

Well, I'm not going to tell you on the first page, am I?

Dan Kelsall

Fucking Good Contents

1. Fuck Fear
Why fear is holding you back from creating good content

2. Fuck Impatience
Why creating effective content takes time, and why you should stop moaning

3. Fuck Marketing
A bit about why marketing is on its arse

4. Fuck Strategy
Why 50-page content strategies are a bag of shit

5. Fuck Campaigns
The only way to build decent campaigns

6. Fuck Money
Why you shouldn't put money behind shit content

7. Fuck the Dark Side
The shady world of dark social and what it means for content marketers

8. Fuck Viral
Why going viral isn't necessarily a good thing

9. Fuck Social Media
Why social media is a pain in the arse for marketers

10. Fuck Brand Awareness
Why brand awareness should never be the focus of any marketing campaign

11. Fuck Collaboration
Why collaborating with others may be bad for you

12. Fuck Leads
Why your content might not bring in any leads

13. Fuck Selling
The reasons you should never, ever sell

14. Fuck Brand Consistency
Why brand consistency is dead and personality is everything

1. FUCK FEAR

The biggest hurdle for most content producers is fear.

Fear of offending customers.

Fear of bad publicity.

Fear of looking stupid.

But it's all bullshit. The fact is, the more unknown your brand, the harder it is to damage it. And you know what? Most of those 'customers' that you're trying so hard not to offend, probably wouldn't buy from you anyway.

But that's not the worst part about producing vanilla shite. The worst part is, for every blog, meme, video, podcast or social media post that you produce that garners no engagement or brings in no new business, you lose money. The time you spent producing that content cost your company.

Most content that people produce is a loss making exercise. Period.

For any content marketing strategy to work, you have to take risks.

You have to try things that your competitors won't. You have to change your tone of voice to something that your industry has never before seen. You have to produce content that adds value to those you want to buy your product.

Make them laugh. Make them cry. Give them knowledge.

But DON'T. FUCKING. SELL.

OK, so it's easy for me to sit here and tell you to take a risk, when I regularly post polarising, mildly (really) offensive content with hashtags like #chocolatedildo, and #walrussex.

I appreciate that if you work for a brand, or you produce content for a client, you can't really get away with the stuff I do. It probably won't go down well if you run an accountancy firm's social media account and you suddenly start tweeting "Philip Hammond's a dickhead." And that's fine. I'm not saying you should.

The level of risk is different in every industry, but one of the things I absolutely guarantee, is that you can push boundaries much, much, much further than you think you can.

It is pushing those boundaries that will make your content stand out. It is pushing those boundaries that'll make your customers sit up and take note.

And, unfortunately, you need to face up to the fact that, when you take a stand, when you say something different, when you stand out, you will get attract criticism. You will attract negativity.

That's part of having a voice.

But if you choose not to have a voice, and you choose to remain dry and corporate, then your audience will become indifferent to your content. They won't care either way.

And that, my little content creators, is fucking poo.

For a marketer, there is nothing worse than indifference.

NOTHING.

#walrussex

When people are indifferent to what you're saying, they'll ignore you. And your brand will remain the same as it always has. Unknown.

Let's think about this book for a second. There are probably more 'fuck's in here than any other business or marketing book. Am I concerned that this will damage my reputation? Nope. I'm comfortable with who I am. I swear in the pub with my mates, I swear in the boardroom. When you do business with me, you get me. Not a professional version of me. Not a diluted version of me. You get the same guy everyone else gets.

You could call it authenticity.

But I hate that word. It lost its meaning because so many people use it without fully understanding what it actually means to be authentic.

Because if you have a 'professional you' and a 'personal you' and maybe a 'you' that only your mates see, then what's real? Which one of those personalities is authentic?

If you have a brand, how can you possibly be authentic when the people representing you are false, 'professional' versions of themselves?

And that, for many people in the business world, is the ultimate risk.

Being yourself is hard. What if you get rejected? What if people don't like you?

Well, there's a little phrase that can help you get over that fear, and that, my chums is, "Fuck 'em."

2. FUCK IMPATIENCE

The reason people aren't able to create brilliant content is generally due to a massive lack of patience.

They expect results yesterday. Not in a week. Not in a month. And if it takes a year, well, fuck that! Am I right?

"I'm not investing in something that takes a year to perfect! I wanna see ROI now."

Well, unfortunately sista, marketing ain't an exact science.

It's a process. Sometimes you'll find something that works right away. Other times you'll be smashing your head against the proverbial brick wall (or literally, if you're a bit mental) trying to come up with your next piece of content.

Even for us naturally creative types, producing stand out content all the time is difficult. Writer's block, or 'creative's block' to be more general, is a pain in the arse.

And, more often than not (and this applies to marketing in general), it is impossible to know for absolute fucking certainty that something – whether that be a post, an article, a video or a whole campaign – will do well.

Analytics will only ever tell you so much.

It doesn't matter how good you think a piece of content is. How well similar pieces have done in the past. How big your following is.

You will NEVER be able to say with complete confidence that that particular piece will set the world alight.

With all marketing, there will always be ups and downs. Peaks and troughs. Hits and misses.

But the bigger your audience gets, the more trust you build, the bigger the hits get and, more importantly, the bigger the misses get. And by bigger I mean, if a hit was 50 comments on an article and a miss was 5 comments, as you grow your audience a hit might be 500 comments, and a miss 50 comments. The misses are now where the original hits were, and probably drive the same results, more often than not.

And if that doesn't make sense, I don't give a shit, because I'm lazy and can't be bothered explaining it again.

But, back to the original point.

If you're not patient with your content, you'll fail. You'll fail to get engagement. You'll fail to grow an audience. And you'll fail to bring in anything tangible from your content marketing.

Getting good at content is about consistently creating, testing, analysing, creating, testing, analysing and so on and so on and so on.

It never stops. And if you're not prepared for that, you might as well give up now.

But don't give up, because I absolutely promise you (and this is something I can say with absolute certainty because I've taught some absolute numpties to do it) that content marketing is not rocket science.

Anyone can build an audience. Anyone can get results.

Might be tomorrow. Might be next month. Might be in ten years. And that's the truth a lot of marketers won't tell you.

Because if they tell you it might take ten years to perfect, you're not going to pay them diddly-dick, are you?

I'll leave this chapter on a final point.

I hate the term 'mentor', but an old bloke who was pretty successful in his field once told me that the difference between entrepreneurs and 'wantrepreneurs' (people who pretend to be entrepreneurs) is that entrepreneurs know in the back of their mind that, no matter what, they will probably never be 'successful'. Given the amount of businesses that fail, they'll probably never 'make it'. But the difference between them and 'wantrepreneurs' is that they'll keep going anyway. When their business fails, they'll still get up the next morning and start all over again. And despite knowing that there's a high chance that they'll be trying and failing until the day they die without ever building anything particularly game changing, they'll still keep at it. They'll keep tweaking, analysing, and trying to better themselves whilst being perfectly comfortable with the fact that success may never come.

Well, it's the same with good content creators.

You may never hit on that career-making campaign. But you keep rolling out of bed and doing it all over again anyway.

Sure, being creative whilst trying to get results is frustrating. Sure, it can be difficult to watch one of your campaigns bomb. Sure, seeing a load of people slag off an article that you've worked on for weeks is painful.

Now I'm not saying that you'll never produce good content, but you need to learn to fall in the love with how fucking tough it is, because it'll never get any easier.

And if not, just go down the route other creatives took to cope with the stresses of producing good material and take drugs or chop off an ear or summat.

#creativestressrelief

3. FUCK MARKETING

There are a multitude of issues with marketing. And by multitude I mean a shit-ton. And by that I mean a bottomless shitty pit of shit problems, covered in shit.

Deep breath

One of those problems stems from the fact that marketing (a bit like recruitment) has such a low barrier to entry. People can literally post on social media once and go, "Right, I'm in marketing now."

Well, you'll never fix that problem, because, unless you're going to start making marketing PHDs a requirement prior to working in marketing, you can't really stop any Tom, Dick or Harry doing it, can you? And I'm not saying there should be a requirement for marketing PHDs because, in my experience, a lot of the time those that have studied marketing via our wonderful education system are normally no better than those with natural talent that haven't. In fact, sometimes those educated folks are worse.

Of course I would say that, because I hold absolutely no quals in marketing. And if that's just stopped you reading this book, that's cool with me. Go and donate it to a charity shop where the word 'fucking' on the front cover will shock the shit out of old ladies whilst they're combing the book shelves for cheap, used, erotic novels.

Anyhoo, the real problem in marketing comes from the fact that most companies don't have a fucking clue what they're doing. And, as a by-product of that, they're contributing to the waves and waves of shit content that permeate our online world. The following will sound very familiar to a lot of you and, if it doesn't, there's a good chance you're lying to yourself, you massive fibber.

The 'We Don't Have a Fucking Clue What We're Doing' Marketing Process:

Hire a marketing person who has a marketing degree that was taught by old blokes that haven't marketed anything since designing WWII propaganda posters.

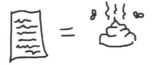

Spend weeks writing a marketing strategy that you don't stick to because it was a pile of shit to begin with.

Set up accounts on every single fucking social channel. "Are you sure we need Instagram to market our incontinence pads, Barry?"

Lose a load of money on PPC, then litter your website and blogs with so many keywords that it doesn't even sound like English anymore, because a 'consultant' told you it's all about the SEO.

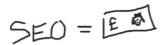

Get absolutely no return on investment because you don't have fucking clue what you're doing, but keep doing it anyway in the hope that, one day, shit "5 ways to..." blogs will become the biggest trend since cat memes.

Sound familiar? Well, I thought I'd put together a really shit diagram to illustrate what I believe the purpose of a marketing function is. Particularly in B2B land.

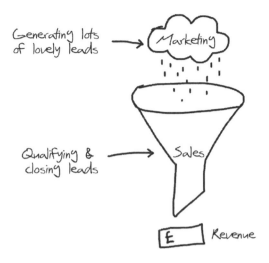

And, in contrast, this, lads and ladettes, is what marketing actually looks like in most establishments. See the problem?

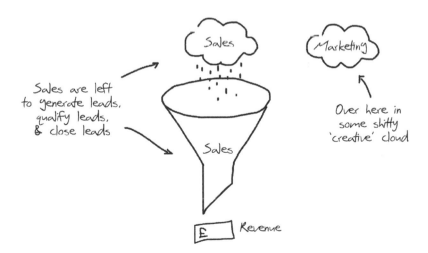

The issue is, marketing is always supposed to generate a return on investment. It's supposed to encourage people to buy from you. But, somewhere along the line, the marketing world became fluffy and began to focus on stuff like 'brand awareness' or 'reach' without actually measuring what that meant for the bottom line. Meanwhile, sales people, who should be focussing on the thing they're good at, closing deals, are spending 80% of their time generating their own leads, whilst marketing smoke crack, roll the bottoms of their chinos up, sip herbal tea and come up with gifs and shit listicles.

What a lot of places need to get back to is marketing that actually brings customers to the table. Imagine what completely inbound would feel like. That's the ideal scenario, right?

Of course, it's unlikely that a business' sales function will ever be entirely inbound. Outbound sales will always have a place in my view. But I honestly believe every business can generate a decent percentage of inbound leads if they get their message right. (Anything past that point relies on your sales team and your product, so don't use this fucking book to beat your marketing peeps around the head if they drive leads that aren't converting because your sales team are pants or you've got a shit product - good marketers aren't miracle workers.)

You see, your marketing team are being paid to bring something to the table. I've worked freelance for years, and have clients from Australia to Holland, and I cannot tell you how many marketing teams I come across that are happy to push out shite, cover their ears, sing "La la la" and ignore the fact that what they're producing is pointless. As far as I'm concerned, they have a responsibility to get results, and contribute to the bottom line, just like everyone else. But first, they need to get your brand's voice right. They need to find a message that works.

One of the best ways to start, is to ask this:

WHAT DO MY CUSTOMERS WANT TO SAY, BUT DAREN'T SAY?

If you can say what they wish they were able to say, you'll immediately garner their admiration and respect.

And what happens when a customer respects you?

They're much more likely to buy from you.

4. FUCK STRATEGY

To build a content strategy, don't build a strategy.

Eh?

Listen, because, and I said this earlier and will probably say it again, going to the trouble of building a strategy before you have any idea what tone of voice, messaging or content works with your audience is nothing short of stupid.

Taking a ridiculous amount of time to write a massive content strategy only to find out that you got it all wrong is, for a marketer, more painful than getting one's genitals trapped in one's zip.

So, the right thing to do (in my opinion, because if I don't say 'in my opinion' I end up looking a bit full of myself, and we don't want that now, do we?) is to test your content first.

Put it this way, if you were developing a product, you wouldn't just go, "Right, here you go customers, have this new, organic, badger-scented eau de toilette!" without testing the market, would you? You'd do a bit of market research to see if people actually wanted to smell like a badger.

Well, it's the same with content.

Sure, at first there's a bit of guesswork involved. It can be hard to know what your market will like, or what stuff will make you or your brand stand out.

Some of you may think you know what your market wants to see, but don't ever assume. And for those that say you can check out other content that does well in your market and replicate it, I say that's fucking lazy.

And by doing that, all you'll ever produce is the same shit everyone else does. There's nothing wrong with being inspired by someone else's content, but that's all it can ever be - inspiration.

If you want to be truly good at content marketing, you need to find things – narratives, tones of voice – that haven't been seen before. And the only way to do that is to try as many different ideas as possible. Most will bomb, but, and this is where it may take a while to get it right, eventually you will stumble upon something that works.

And here's where most people get it wrong. They keep producing content and when they stumble upon something good, a message or subject or whatever, that works, they pat themselves on the back, have a fucking biscuit, and then never do anything like it again.

But you, as a content creator, don't have the right to decide when your market's had enough of a particular type of content. The analytics will tell you when they've had enough.

Let's say you have a couple of posts about a subject – say the gender pay gap - that do well. There's so much you can say around that subject that you should probably try and build a campaign around it (more about that later).

You've stumbled upon something that your target audience want to see and, unless your market's proper niche, there will be tons more of your target audience out that will probably react positively to something similar.

Make sense?

The point is, your content strategy is a live document. You should be prepared to change anything and everything from one day to the next. But if you write a 50-page document and something changes tomorrow which fucks that entire document over, you've got to write a new 50-page document, and that's stupid.

And the other thing that massively pisses me off about these huge marketing documents is, no-one ever really sticks to them anyway, which makes them even more pointless. If you're a CMO or marketing manager or whatever, and you honestly think your team have gone through and digested all the crap you included in your boring, little plan, you're kidding yourself.

The stuff they do stick to is the proper literal bits like, "We're going to post an industry tip on our Instagram each day, designed like this, and written in this tone of voice, and at this time," and then your team continue to push that out each day, but it gets no engagement and drives no traffic etc. but they keep doing it because it was part of this big, rigid, crappy strategy that you came up with.

Not one of you tested whether your market wanted to see those shitty tips and, what baffles me even more is the fact that you'll probably be pushing out those shitty industry tips for the next 6 months, and not one of you will say, "These are fucking pointless. We're wasting our time." So bin the strategies off. Get good at one thing, get your message right, find out what works with your audience and begin to build a loose plan around it.

I'm not saying content strategies shouldn't exist. What I'm saying is, they're something you build over time and constantly adapt based on what your market wants to see.

5. FUCK CAMPAIGNS

Right, so what's a campaign then?

Well, it's just basically taking a message that works with your target market (which you'll only find by testing different messages), and getting organised around it.

It's about planning a series of content, for one or more channels, to be executed over a period of time. Which sounds simple, but it's not really. And it can be frustrating.

So, say you find that a tweet you wrote, taking the piss out of Richard Branson's weird, yellow hair, did well. You had thousands of likes and retweets, your followers sky rocketed and it even brought in bit of business. You might then decide that your brand will now try a campaign around taking the piss out of other successful entrepreneurs in the hope that it will attract the same engagement, bring in even more followers and net you some more custom.

Only it doesn't.

You see, just because a message did well, it doesn't mean your campaign will. Now, I know I said earlier that good campaigns are built around messages that you found to work, but the truth is, it doesn't matter how well a message in a piece of content did, there's nothing to say your target market will react in the same way to it when they see more of it. There's always a chance it was a one-hit-wonder.

Not only that, but many topics are time sensitive too. That's why when you find a message that works, you can't spend 6 months dicking around creating a campaign around it. You need to work quickly, because I guarantee, someone will beat you too it.

Not only is content hit and miss, campaigns are too. Get comfortable with that fact and know that, just because a particular campaign was a flop, it doesn't mean the next one will be. Get back to trying different kinds of content, find something that works and go again. It's frustrating, but this is where that patience comes in.

Oh, and always analyse your content. Work out what went well, what had the highest percentage of engagement from your target audience, and what hit your key metrics – revenue, users, hires, whatever.

Keep track of high performing campaigns because, although you'll never know for definite that a content campaign will do well, campaigns that mimic those that did well previously have a higher chance of garnering the same results. I don't need to explain why. That's just common sense, Susan.

People always ask me, "Should we include other channels in our campaigns?"

My answer is always the same: Only if you think you've got the time to manage other channels.

What do I mean by that?

Well, let's say you've got a new office dog accessory brand. Let's call it 'Office Shit Bags'. You noticed a gap in the market because everyone nowadays seems to think that an office dog is the answer to a happy workforce, so you started creating little customisable, branded poo bags. You manage to grow a decent Instagram page and sales are coming in steadily. You find that your best performing content is pics of office dogs curling one out on fake grass, under Ping-Pong tables or next to beanbags, so you want to build a campaign around it. You also want to replicate the success you've had on Insta on other channels, so you set up a Facebook page. You quickly realise that building an audience on Facebook is completely different to Instagram, and you struggle to get to grips with paid ad campaigns. It takes time to constantly produce content, most of which doesn't work, and your following is taking ages to grow. Meanwhile, your Insta page has taken a hit because, in between fulfilling orders, creating content, dealing with invoicing, and your new FB channel, you haven't had the time to concentrate on it. And, because of that, you're now getting less sales. A month later, your company goes bust, your partner leaves you, and you starve to death.

Do you get my point?

If you're a small business and you don't have the time to master another channel, don't try it. Wait until your main channel is bringing in enough leads or customers, and either take on someone else to free up some of your time so that you can put the required effort into building another channel, or use the increase in cash to outsource the building of your second channel to an agency who knows what they're doing.

The worst thing you can do as a marketer is overstretch yourself. Being creative is tough, especially when you're drained. If you take on too much, your creativity will take a battering, your content will go back to being shit, and, voila, you're back at square one.

As I said earlier, patience is everything.

6. FUCK MONEY

Right, so we're all precious about the stuff that we create. We're all protective of our ideas. It's only natural.

But the problem with that is, if we create something and it doesn't do well, we often hold onto it. That's why marketing teams continue to push out the same corporate videos, or entrepreneurs stick with their crappy podcasts and keep inviting guests on, despite the fact that after 17 episodes, they still only attract an average of 2 listeners.

In the same way that it's hard for a mother to look at their child and think they're ugly, even if they have a face like a bulldog licking piss off a nettle, when we create stuff, it's hard to view it negatively. After all, we put our blood sweat and tears into it. It can't be bad.

So when we push out a piece of content and it dives, our automatic reaction isn't to think, "well, that was turd." Instead, (and we're all guilty of this) we make excuses. We say stuff like, "[insert social media platform of choice]'s algorithm screwed me over" or " I released it at the wrong time of day" or one of a vast array of other things we say to defend our creations.

But in reality, the reason that piece of content didn't do well is because, in truth, it wasn't very good.

However, rather than admit that fact, do you know what a lot of marketing teams and content creators do?

They put money behind it.

And do you know what happens to that money?

It gets swallowed up by the online, money-gobbling machine, never to be seen again.

Think about it.

If a piece of content goes out to your target audience and gets little to no engagement, do you honestly think that by pushing it via a paid campaign, you'll somehow convince others in your target audience that it's worth engaging with?

What do you think the chances of that are?

The point is, you have an opportunity on most channels to test your content with your market.

For free.

And only when you find a piece of content that works should you put money behind it.

Because a piece of content that does well with your target audience organically will probably also do well with more of your target audience if you build a paid campaign around it.

It's not the most complicated theory to get your noggin around, is it?

If you find something that works well organically prior to every paid campaign, what do you think will happen to your success rate?

That's right. There's a good chance it'll improve.

Simple, init?

7. FUCK THE DARK SIDE

Okay, so I know I go on all the time about tracking everything and measuring the impact of every piece of content, and tracking your target audience percentage and blah blah, fucking blah.

But there's a bit of an issue.

It's a little thing called 'dark social'.

Sounds sinister, doesn't it?

Well, lads and gentleladies, 'dark social' is a marketer's worst nightmare.

So what the hell is it?

It's the fact that, no matter what tools you use to measure the impact of your content, or how well you know your way around Google Analytics, you will never be able to know the origin of every bit of traffic. And, actually, some sources suggest you'll never truly know the origin of MOST of your traffic. Instead, it usually just gets lumped in with 'direct traffic' which isn't very fair, is it?

But how come?

Well, the nature of t'internet, means that your customers may see your content via a hidden channel. And what I mean by that is, unless you're a government hacker who spies on people through their webcam and stuff, your little analytics application can't pick up private activity.

So when little Susie shares your post about the intricacy of gender neutrality in otters with her mate via Whatsapp and her

mate visits your site via that link, you've no idea where that traffic came from.

But, in truth, there's absolutely nothing you can do about it. And the less people publicly share content, the more of your traffic goes 'dark'.

The only thing you can hope to do is marry up content with spikes in visits to your social pages, profiles or website. Although it's not massively accurate, you can usually assume that a certain spike was caused by a particular piece of content.

"So I'm going to be guessing forever then?"

To a certain extent, Bob, yeah. GDPR was a big, fat, painful thorn in the marketing industry's side. I mean, it's a good thing, protecting people's privacy and stuff, but the fact that social platforms have locked down a shitload of their APIs means that it's very hard to get access to any meaningful data. You'll find that many of the tools and dashboards available to social media marketers are fucking useless if you actually drill down into the tangible value they provide. Most of them are just churning out analytics that are freely available on the platforms themselves.

Combine that with dark social, and it doesn't paint a very 'insightful' future, does it? But hey, we've got to work with what we've got. And if you think it's bad now (a study by RadiumOne in 2014 suggested 70% of referrals come from 'dark social' - if that's anything to go by, it'll be higher now), I guarantee that things are only going to get worse. People are going to be sharing things privately more and more, and the tighter we get with data, the less insights we'll get as marketers.

Tough cookies, mate.

8. FUCK VIRAL

So I spent a lot of time trying to go viral, and helped many clients do it too.

The aim was simple. Make as much fucking noise as possible, and drive masses of traffic that I could then manipulate into buying products or services. Basically similar to the model a few digital agencies use, where they build or acquire viral channels and leverage them for other brands.

Don't get me wrong. Going viral is hard work. And until you've built up a decent following, going viral repeatedly is pretty much impossible.

Viral content generally looks like the following: pick a subject with mass-market appeal, make sure it's written in an engaging way, and time it right. (If it's already been overdone, it probably won't work.) Oh, and the bigger your audience or following, the more likely you are to go viral. Obviously. The more often you go viral, the bigger your audience becomes, and the more likely you are to continue going viral.

But, after spending a shedload of time creating content for myself and clients in different industries with the aim of going viral and attracting new customers, I realised something.

Many of the leads seemed to be coming from the posts that didn't do as well. The ones tailored to a niche audience.

Now, you're probably thinking, fuck me, Dan, every marketer knows that. But do they though? Would companies really be spending so much money with viral influencers if they truly knew that?

So, I decided to drill down into the figures to see which posts brought in the most business. My suspicions were right. In quite a few cases, the viral posts brought in less leads.

We created a tool that was able to scrape the engagement from social posts, so that I could see the breakdown of my audience. A bit naughty as I'm accessing data that the social networks don't want me to have (Yup, I'm a GDPR criminal), but it was the only way to truly know.

You see, the problem with going organically viral is that you can't really determine where that content goes, and who sees it. And the more mass market it is and the more it spreads, the more likely it is to get engagement from those outside of your target audience. And, when you're looking for business, that's not a good thing. It's dangerous in two ways:

1) You'll increase your following, but they'll be the wrong people (not your potential customers) and it will dilute your audience.

2) The next time you post, it will appear on the feeds of the wrong people and guess what? No business.

What I found was, for the viral posts that drove few leads, a high percentage of those engaging with the content weren't my target audience.

And, while we're on the subject of going viral, let me tell you about something else I learnt via a decision I made this year.

LinkedIn decided to introduce measures that would stop what they considered to be 'unprofessional' content on the platform. They introduced a reporting function, and encouraged 'members' to actively flag posts that they considered unprofessional.

Get enough people reporting your post and, boom. Bye, bye content. Get a shed load of people reporting you regularly and you can kiss goodbye to your reach. It's nothing new. Twitter, Instagram, and Facebook have all shut down pages and accounts, and censored content.

LinkedIn is no different.

There are also rumours (and this is my worst) that they've added bots to actively scan LI content for profanity. And if they stumble across a 'fuck,' 'shit' or 'bollocks' then once again, au revoir reach or, sometimes, that piece of content will disappear for good. In total, I've lost 12 pieces of content. I'm aiming for 50, and then I'll write a book called, 'What Not to Post on LinkedIn'.

So here's the thing.

Despite the platform being the social media equivalent of North Korea, my point here isn't just to whinge about LinkedIn - their platform, their rules after all - it's to show you what really matters when it comes to content.

You see, I spent a good year going repeatedly viral. The issue was, every piece of my content, like this book, was littered with swearing and weird, often crude, analogies. Some said I did it to stand out, others labelled it as a form of attention seeking, but, in truth, it's just because, in real life, I swear. A lot. And yeah, it certainly helps me stand out from other content marketers.

When I stumbled upon the news of LinkedIn censorship, I had a choice. Knock the naughty words on the head, something of a trademark of mine, and start writing like the 'professionals' do, or say, 'fuck you LinkedIn,' carry on the way I was and risk my reach being affected or some gimpy job's worth taking down my posts.

I took the latter approach.

Suicide for a marketer, right?

Not exactly. You see, I already knew that my viral posts brought me in less business. I was already well aware that my niche posts were my bread and butter. And I'd already built up a big enough audience of the right people that, even if my reach were limited, it would still hit a decent enough percentage of my target audience to generate business.

So, I continued with the swearing and the weird analogies. I stuck to my guns. And, sure enough, my reach was affected. My engagement dropped. Prior to LinkedIn siding with the easily offended, according to our tool I hit an average of 2400 likes and 300 comments per post. In just a couple of months, that average slid to 1100 likes and 150 comments. And my profile views dipped significantly.

But you know what? The amount of leads I get through has been on the up ever since.

Interesting, init?

Now, I'm not saying that going viral is pointless. If your product or service is suitable for the mass market, or if a large percentage of the users of a certain social channel are your target audience, going viral works a treat. And though I'm not an advocate of using 'brand awareness' as a focus of any content marketing, I can't deny that viral content is the quickest way to get your name out there.

But remember, the whole point of content marketing is to be consistent; to build an audience that repeatedly engages with you so that, when they come to buy, you're the first person or brand that they think about. You're much better off getting 200 likes and 20 comments on every post from a core group of people than getting 20000 likes and 2000 comments once every so often and getting fuck all engagement on each post in between. Going viral occasionally isn't how you build a brand.

Consistent engagement from the same people. And the more people you get looking out for, and engaging with your stuff, the bigger your audience gets. That's how you build trust. That's how you nurture fans. That's how you win new customers with your content.

Another thing I want to address here, are the marketers and digital agencies that have taken to labelling high engagement numbers as 'vanity metrics'.

In a lot of cases, high numbers are just that. Getting 10,000 likes from peeps in China or India if your product is only suitable for a UK market is useless. Just check out that bloke, Oleg, on LinkedIn for an example of pointless content.

However, you'll also notice that those who label high engagement as 'vanity metrics' are often the ones who get very little engagement on their own content.

You see, going viral can be good or bad. It's the lack of control that's the problem. On the plus side, high numbers not only do a lot for raising your profile, but if you look at them closely, sometimes they can be beneficial.

Check out this shite diagram:

A.

34 likes, 3 comments

↓

17 likes & 2 comments
from target audience

↓

51% target audience

B.

3,400 likes, 300 comments

↓

247 likes & 19 comments
from target audience

↓

7% target audience

So, let's compare post A and post B. On the surface, you might think post A has a better target audience percentage (which is all some marketing tools might tell you), so therefore, it must be the better piece of content. But, actually, post B has miles more engagement from your target audience - the lower percentage is just a result of having higher numbers. But what about if you produced 10 pieces of content - 5 posts matched post A's performance, and 5 matched post B's. And even though group 'B' had appealed to more of your target audience, group 'A' brought in more leads. Group 'A' might be niche content, tailored specifically to your target customer, hence the lower engagement, and group 'B' might be mass market content, so naturally resonated with a wide variety of people, including people who happened to be your target audience. And because it was mass market content, those in your target audience who reacted to it didn't realise what it is you or your company do, didn't visit your profile or website and, therefore, didn't become aware of what you do, let alone buy.

The point is, you can never assume a piece of content or campaign is good or bad, based on high or low numbers alone.

However, it's important to note that, although a piece of content with low engagement like post A can be good, or even a campaign of posts with low engagement, you'll only ever build a large audience quickly if you get large numbers. Never underestimate herd mentality. Never underestimate how influenced people are by brands and/or people that attract a lot of engagement and a large following.

And lastly, it's important to take into account how social media works here, particularly when it comes to viral content. You see, likes and comments are the currency of social. If a piece of content gets low numbers, it only reached a small number of people. If it only reached a small number of people, that means it only reached a small number of your target audience.

Remember, every time someone likes or comments on your content, whether that person is part of your target audience or not, one of two things happens:

1) It appears in the feeds of that person's followers, and some of those may also be your target audience (some networks are slightly different) or;

2) It's featured by the social network you posted it on due to being popular and having high numbers, which also means that it will naturally reach more of your target audience.

Like I said, there's a real lack of control with organic viral content, but that doesn't mean that it isn't valuable.

And as a side note, don't forget: negative comments by double-hard keyboard warriors have the exact same effect. When someone attacks you, just laugh at the fact that they've contributed to the popularity of your content. Fucking morons.

9. FUCK SOCIAL MEDIA

So I've already mentioned how quickly social media platforms change. You might find that something that works really well today, doesn't work tomorrow. One change in an algorithm can upend your entire social strategy. One change in social media policies can result in the removal or censoring of content or, god forbid, a ban on that account you've worked to build up for the past few years.

Just look what happened to half the Twitter parody accounts in 2015. One change to Twitter's policies and off they fucked to the social media bin. Take the 'Broetry' style LinkedIn posts of 2017, led by some bloke called Josh. They used to hit the tens of thousands for a good few months. But then they dived. A combination of changes to the platform and audiences getting fed up of the double-spaced, made up stories meant that those that grew huge audiences with that type of content saw their engagement fall off a cliff.

The point is, you can never assume that something will always work. And there is absolutely nothing you can do to prevent changes happening. It's out of your control.

And because of that, guess what?

There is NO SUCH THING AS A SOCIAL MEDIA EXPERT.

Yup. You heard me.

Now, there might be a few of you getting a bit pissy after reading that. You might be the type who describes yourself as an expert. 'Facebook Expert' or 'Instagram Guru' might even be your job title. But when something changes as quick as social media, there is absolutely no way anyone is an expert.

The only difference between good social media marketers and shit ones is, the former keep on top of the constant changes and the latter are still hanging onto stuff that worked 5 years ago.

But you cannot describe yourself as an 'expert' if one change tomorrow means that you need to figure out what works all over again. Even if you're good at it. In fact, I'll let you off if you change your job title to 'Social Media Expert For The Time Being'.

The amount of LinkedIn experts and consultants that somehow manage to sell their services to loads of people, despite getting little engagement on their own content, is ridiculous.

If you're looking for a marketer - whether 3rd party or to hire - ask yourself this:

How good are they at marketing themselves?

If they're an Instagram 'expert' and have less than 10k followers, ask yourself why. If they're a LinkedIn 'guru' and get 10 likes a post, ask yourself if they're really who they say they are. Marketing is full of charlatans. If they can't market themselves well, that's your first sign that they're probably shite.

Another thing that I need to address in this section is around the importance of keeping things native to each platform. What I mean by that is, you need to create pieces of content specifically for each social media channel that you use.

As an example, you need to stop sharing YouTube links on LinkedIn.

Why?

Well, let's think about it.

The purpose of any social media platform is to keep you, the user, on it for as long as possible. The longer you, and your audience for that matter, are there, the more money the platform makes.

So, LinkedIn introduced a native video function so that you can upload your own videos about deaf, homeless kids with half a face who became billionaires because they got up at 5am and crushed it. When users watch your native video, they remain on the platform.

However, when you share a link to another social media platform, like YouTube, that naturally draws users away from LinkedIn and, for obvious reasons, LinkedIn don't like that, fam.

And so they put measures in place to limit the reach of such shares, because they don't want you directing users to their competitors. They want to keep people in a 'scroll hole' and anyone encouraging people to leave the platform is essentially taking money from them.

What I'm saying is, the old 'let's share links all over the place' tactic is dead. You need to take the time to create specific content for each platform that you use or, at the very least, reformat and natively upload your existing content.

Transferring your audience to other channels is harder than it used to be, but you won't have an audience to transfer if your content's reach is limited by the fact that you keep posting outside links.

10. FUCK BRAND AWARENESS

Brand awareness, as a business goal, is bollocks.

Seriously.

If you're an SME, or a startup, and you get 2 likes on each piece of content you produce, what brand awareness?

No one has a fucking clue who you are.

One of the major issues with the digital marketing industry is the number of agencies that sell marketing campaigns with a focus on 'brand awareness'. They get you to chuck a load of money behind rubbish material that get's a few thousand 'views' and then pat themselves on the back on what they tell you was a job well done.

"Look at the reach!" they'll say. But, ladies and gentlemen, if it brought in no new customers, or no revenue, or it didn't increase your userbase, 'reach' means diddly squat.

Brand awareness comes as a by-product of producing good content. Brand awareness develops as a result of consistently winning new business.

Large brands, that control a substantial market share, are the only companies that have the time, and budget, to run 'brand awareness' campaigns.

Why?

Because it's about retention. Their brand names are engrained in their industries. Staying at the forefront of the consumer's mind is really fucking important.

But you, the smaller brand, whom nobody knows about, can't stay at the forefront of your customer's mind when you were never in their mind in the first place.

Forget about brand awareness for now. You need to produce content that gets results.

Right, I know the fact that I'm slagging off brand awareness campaigns is going to piss off a lot of traditional marketers.

But the focus shouldn't be on reach. High reach numbers come as a result of driving engagement.

But it's important to note here that engagement is changing.

Share figures are dropping all over the show. Seriously. Reports even suggest that Buzzfeed, one of the most popular content channels on the planet at the minute, are experiencing a huge drop in the number of people sharing their content.

But engagement figures aren't slowing. People are just engaging in a different way. They're having conversations instead in the comments on posts. They're tagging their mates in. And on platforms like Instagram, users don't want to share someone else's content to their own account. That's where the stuff they've personally created lives. It's miles easier, and preferable, to quickly tag their pals under a meme they know they'd appreciate, rather than litter their own social media with someone else's content. Or, and we touched on 'dark social' earlier, they'll share it via a private message.

It works exactly the same in B2B. I'm sorry, but nobody's sharing those shitty blogs on your website to their personal social channels. You might as well get rid of that outdated 'Share on Twitter' button.

f Share

Here lies the share b

Gone but never forg

2004 - 2019

#RIPsharebutton

And less and less people are pressing the share button on LinkedIn, in the realisation that it adds absolutely no real value whatsoever. They're becoming increasingly aware that a comment is a miles better way to show their appreciation to the author.

People used to say that you had to create 'shareable' content for it to have any chance of going viral. But that's no longer the case. Nowadays, it's about driving conversations. Provoking debate. Causing a stir under the content itself. The algorithms of social platforms will do the rest.

So stop worrying about reach. Stop telling your employees and mates to share your posts and articles. Instead focus on consistently creating good content that encourages conversations and debate.

The awareness of your brand will grow as a by-product.

11. FUCK LEADS

Wait, what?

Fuck leads?

"But, Dan, you've been harping on throughout this entire book about how marketing people are shit if they don't bring in anything tangible."

Which is true.

But that doesn't necessarily mean leads. Well, not at first anyway.

Put it this way. How many times have you made a purchase after reading a social media post? Rarely, right? How about a blog post on a website? Same?

Now, when it comes to B2C, I'm pretty sure tons of people make purchases when they watch videos from their favourite influencers, because the we all know the general public are a bit dim and can't make decisions for themselves, but it's a little different when it comes to B2B.

Because when it's a business purchase, it's never an impulse buy, is it? It's generally pretty measured. They need to know miles more about you before deciding to pick up that phone, or fill in an enquiry form on your website, never mind part with some of that tiny budget that they only got after pulling the ops director with the hairy mole and yellow pits at the Christmas party.

And because of that fact, it can take a while to convince them to buy. That's why, when you first start releasing content into the wild, you can't suddenly expect the leads to come rolling in.

It's important to measure your success in other ways. At least at first. Otherwise, you're going to get pissed off very quickly.

Like what?

Well, engagement at first. Although engagement doesn't mean success exactly, it's still critical when you're building an audience. If you're getting a decent amount of engagement, the numbers are consistent, and a good amount of those engaging with your content are your target market, that's something to celebrate. You're well on your way to building an audience. Pat yourself on the head and have a fruit pastille.

Next, is that resulting in an increase in activity elsewhere? More profile or page visits on social, rising follower numbers, more website visits, an increase in subscriptions to your newsletter? Remember, if more people are checking out what you do, that's a good sign.

Another thing to keep note of is whether people are actively reaching out. Are you getting private messages from people in your target market telling you how they love your content? Are they tagging you in posts? Sharing your articles? Sending little packages to your house with drugs and used underwear in? All of these things are positive.

Past that, it's important to remember that sometimes converting leads isn't as simple in some industries as it is in others.

I'm in content marketing, so when I write a piece of content that does well, I am literally displaying my services directly. I don't have to talk about what it is I do. I just do it and, as a by-product of creating a good piece of content, I get regular leads.

It's not that simple if you sell software, or office sanitary bins.

You see, what some of you might need to do is be a bit more proactive, and continue conversations with those that reach out to you, or that engage with your content regularly.

If you strike a chord with someone and you get to the point of discussing your product, it's either time to meet, or time to pass them over to your sales guys if you're a bigger business.

But again, you shouldn't need to sell here. If you're having real conversations with your target market, and taking a genuine interest in what they have to say, that should naturally lead onto talking about your product or service eventually.

The point of this bit is to get you to realise that content marketing is a process. You can't expect a ton of leads from a few months of posting stuff on LinkedIn, or writing a couple of articles on Medium.

Be happy with the small wins first.

12. FUCK COLLABORATION

OK, so I might step on a few toes with this one, but collaborations with other content creators are only good sometimes.

Trust me, I've made this mistake enough to know.

The thing is, it's all well and good being asked to do a podcast, be featured in some interview, or contribute to an article. It's flattering almost.

But there are several things you need to consider before doing this.

Firstly, does the person producing the content have their own audience? Do they get a lot of engagement or listeners or whatever? If they're releasing podcast episodes every week, but their listener numbers aren't increasing, and each time they push it out on social nobody really engages with it, you need to ask yourself whether it's worth doing. I understand the value from their perspective. Chances are, you'll share it because you're featured in it, and that in turn with attract your audience to their content. But that does far more for them than it does for you.

I'll give you an example. I push out content 1-2 times a week. I get around 5-10 leads per week. Minimal effort, and a pretty decent return. I don't really need to do anything else to keep the business growing at a steady rate. However, if somebody else with a decent audience approaches me with the chance to do a video or podcast, it probably makes sense. I can tap into their audience and further grow my personal brand, whilst they can tap into my audience and further grow their own. But there's little point in me spending valuable time collaborating with people who don't already have an audience, because it won't really help me grow any faster.

Sounds big headed, doesn't it?

But what you have to realise is, we're all here to make money. We all have limited time and, when it comes to marketing, the bigger and more engaged your audience is, the more valuable that time is. Giving it away willy nilly is daft.

Now I'm not saying don't help other people out. Occasionally, that's cool. But if you're spending half your time recording podcasts for completely unknown channels and sharing the content of people that don't have an audience, not only will it not add anything to your own marketing efforts, but it can actually be detrimental to them.

Why? Because, like I said earlier, being creative is hard. Anything that takes away from your own creative efforts has to be worth it. Rather than spending a day contributing to someone's shit article that nobody's going to read, you could be putting those efforts into creating a quality bit of content for your own channel.

And I guarantee that if you start sharing shit content with your audience just because you were featured in it and you feel like you owe the person that created it, they'll begin to get sick of it. They'll move on to someone or some brand that they find more interesting. Audiences are fickle. If you start pushing out garbage, they'll drop you quicker than if someone handed them a pair of anal beads and said, "They've just been up John Prescott's arse, mate."

So, content creators, get a bit selfish. The bigger your audience gets, the more collaboration requests you'll get.

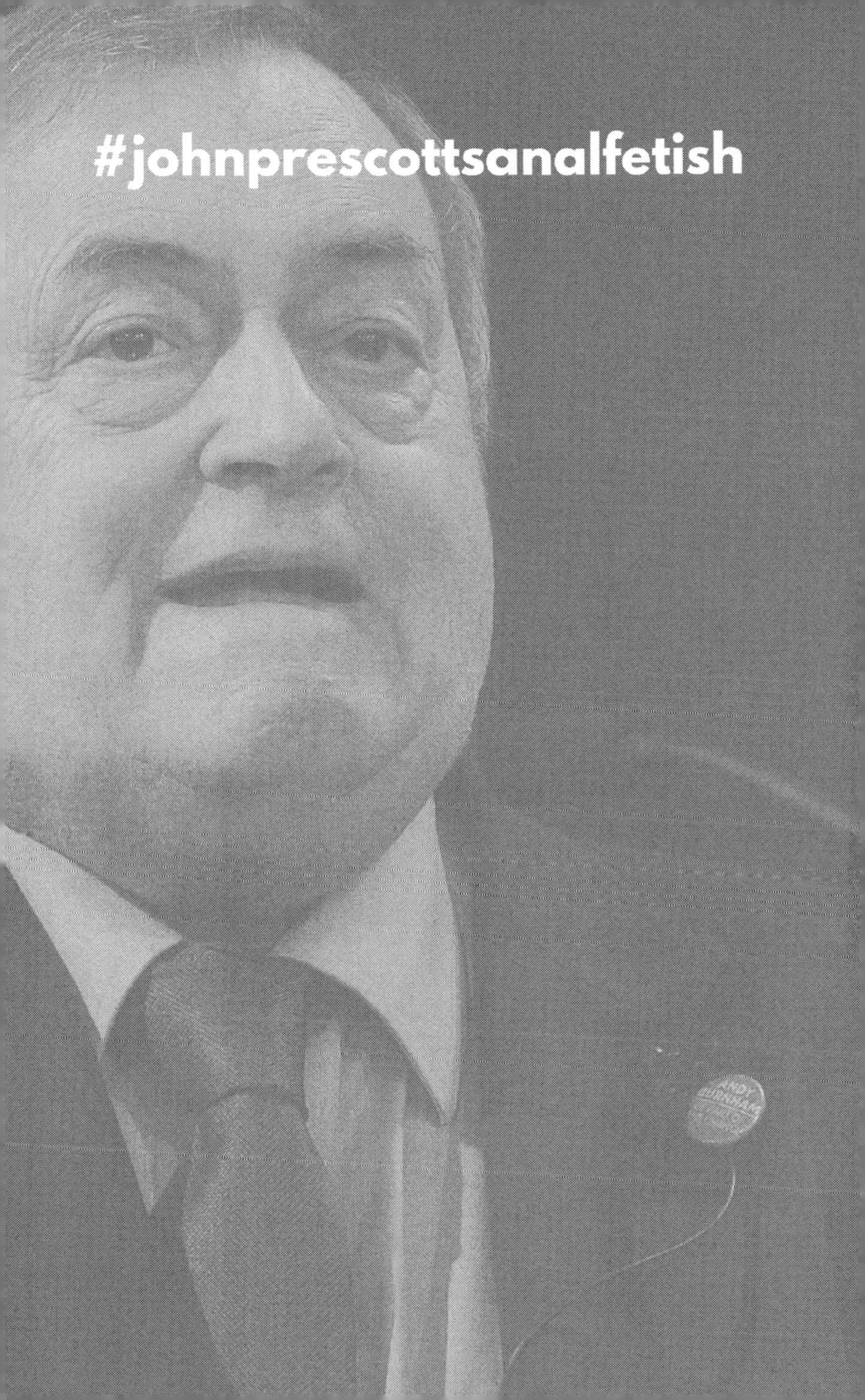
#johnprescottsanalfetish

13. FUCK SELLING

Put your hand up if you like being cold-called?

Anyone? No?

How about spammed over email?

What about getting stopped in the street by some gimpy student trying to get you to donate a quid a month to a charity that gives wigs to children born without shins?

I thought not.

Well, it's exactly the same when all you put out on social media is stuff about how your company's anal bleaching kit is better than your competitor's.

Nobody gives a shit. People hate being sold to. But, guess what?

People like to buy.

"So, people want to buy but I can't sell to them? Fuck's sake, Dan, you better start making sense or I'm going to roundhouse you in the testicles."

I know. It's hard to get your head around. The thing is, people don't like pressure. They want to buy when they're ready.

So, instead of selling, the smart move is to produce content that resonates with your target audience. Content that provides value, fosters debate and, by saying something your customers wish they could say, helps you to build trust, respect and admiration within your market.

And when those customers are ready to buy, where do they go?

To a brand, or individual, that they trust, A.K.A you.

Make sense?

Because they'd rather buy off you. It's the old cliché, 'people buy people'.

You see, no one trusts brands anymore. Particularly not new ones. That's another reason branded content never does particularly well. It feels contrived. It feels like no matter what a brand pushes out, they're always trying to sell.

Everyone's big on 'personal brands' at the minute.

And I agree. The way to rocket your B2B marketing efforts is to forget about your brand for the time being, and use your people.

Use their personalities to build different, smaller audiences within your target market. If their content hits the right people, your customers will find your brand, and products, as a consequence of the mint stuff they produce.

The problem is, however, people get it so fucking wrong. Most attempts at personal branding involve posting motivational quotes and plagiarising other people's content.

But you're not the motivational love child of Tony Robbins and Gary Vee. You're you.

And there is stuff you can say that will massively appeal to people within your target audience. It doesn't have to appeal to everyone in your target audience, though.

That's the beauty of having multiple personalities putting out content.

Different parts of your market will be drawn to the different people in your organisation.

And they'll buy off them. They don't have to like you all.

It only takes a prospect to like one of you, to buy into one of you, to resonate with the content that one of you pushes out, to decide to start a conversation, or even to make a purchase.

Gary Vaynerchuk

You

Tony Robbins

14. FUCK BRAND CONSISTENCY

Marketers used to believe that all B2B content had to be branded. "Brand consistency", they used to call it. But it's bullshit. Having the same colour and rubbish spiel on every piece of content you produce won't bring in business.

Marketing has changed. The people within your company will have opinions. Knowledge. Stories to tell. Stuff that will resonate with your target audience. Well, some of them will anyway.

There will also be people in your business that are about as about as interesting as a Friday night in watching repeats of University Challenge with a falafel wrap and a glass of water. They're probably not the best choice as content producers.

And of course you can have a bit of the branded stuff. But without an audience, who the fuck'll read it?

Like I said earlier. The brand sits behind those people. It's on their social profiles. It's subtly placed at the end of ebooks. And it'll be found if they're pushing out top quality content to your target customers. Their job is to capture little pockets of your market. To create small audiences that love the stuff they have to say.

Why? Because they'll like the cut of an employee's jib, see amazing content from them all the time, and go and check out what it is they do. Even if that customer isn't ready to buy yet, they'll be aware of your product or service and, when the time's right, they'll buy.

Let's go back to the point I made earlier about how you'll never get 'everyone' to buy from you.

It's impossible.

What you want is to attract the customers that are like you. Their values are the same, their opinions similar, and their business objectives mimic your own.

Why? Because, in short, it's miles easier to work with customers you gel with than those you don't.

So, what's the best way to attract a likeminded audience to your content?

Yep, you guessed it. Be yourself.

"But what if I put myself out there, and people don't like me? What if I piss some potential customers off?"

So what? How do you know they'd buy from you in the first place? And, if they did, I'd guess that if they're not the type of person you'd get on with, chances are they're likely to become a difficult customer.

They won't get your jokes. They won't resonate with the stuff you say. They'll be harder to talk around when things go tits up. And this is business. Things always go tits up.

By producing content that attracts potential customers that are like you, you'll begin to build an audience. The more that audience grows, the more likely others are to notice. And eventually, your company's brand will surpass your personal brand, and whether or not people like you won't matter anymore.

Plenty of people don't like Branson, but it doesn't stop them using that shite train service, does it?

In fact, this is probably the wankiest thing that I've ever written, but people need to stop trying to be Virgin, and be Branson instead.

Actually, fuck that. FUCK. THAT.

Now please excuse me whilst I go and have a cold shower.

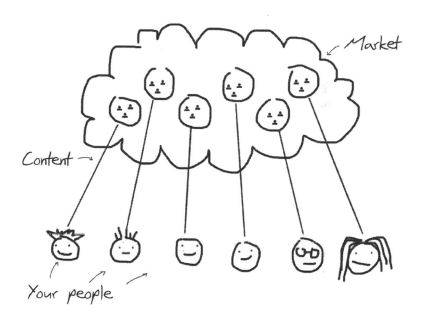

15. FUCK SCHEDULING TOOLS

Hootsuite. Buffer. TweetDeck. We could go on for ages.

For years, when it came to social media content, scheduling your posts was the thing to do. It'd save time, ensure consistency, make sure that your account was regularly active, and allow you to concentrate on more 'important' things.

But most of the time, the best content is reactive. At least to a certain extent. It plays on the 'now', not the '2 months ago'. You can't create current content, weeks in advance. In fact, I'd argue that this 'schedule-and-forget-it' mentality is one of the most detrimental things you can do when it comes to content creation. Why is content seen as something that you need to get out of the way? Of all marketing, it is categorically the most import bit; the one thing everyone needs to get right before doing anything else.

Still not buying it?

I tell you what, let's address each of the 'advantages' of scheduling tools one by one, shall we?

1. They save time.

Yes and no. It saves time in the short term. But in the long run, you'll have produced so much shit content that you won't get anywhere near the results you could have had, if only you'd spent a bit more time each week pushing out less content, but of a higher quality. There ain't a tool out there that can automate that for you, unfortunately.

2. They help you post consistently.

Yeah. They can. But my argument here is that posting old, badly produced content regularly is, more often than not, about as good as not posting at all.

3.   They allow you to concentrate on more important things.

What's more important than content? Pulling your plonker? If your content's shit, it'll negatively affect everything else. Do you think your paid ads will be as effective with shit messaging? Do you reckon your social account will be growing as quick as it could if every post is exactly the same as the crap your competition put out?

I get it. It's hard work thinking of good content all the time. You'd rather create and automate posts for the next 3 months in bulk, leaving you more time to read stuff like this crappy book. But the thing is, your entire strategy rests upon your content.

Shit content, shit marketing.

Simple as that, love.

16. FUCK OPINIONS

Like with parenting, or football, or how to become 'successful', everyone has an opinion.

And that's fine to a certain extent.

But, whether you're a client, or a creative, or a founder of a startup, or a marketing director or anyone else for that matter, 90% of the ideas that you come up with will be shit. And they'll fail. In fact, probably more than 90%.

That's why, for the most part, opinions mean nothing when it comes to marketing.

Let's say you've built a new website, and you and your copywriter are arguing about the landing page text. You can spend all day bickering about what will and won't work, but you only ever really know what will work when it actually does.

Let me say that again.

When it comes to marketing, you will never know for certain whether something will work until it does.

Shit that, isn't it.

So your opinion, and the argument you're having with your copywriter, is pointless. Just test both ideas. And then, when one works better than the other, you or your copywriter can be a wanker and give it the ol', "Told you so."

Now, there are a growing number of people touting the use of 'web psychology' and 'neuroscience' in marketing or, more specifically, content marketing. They claim that there are ways of knowing what makes your target audience tick and, therefore, knowing what they'll react well too. That should then mean that there's a good chance they'll know which bits of content will do well, and which won't. No need for opinions at all, right?

And that's all well and good in theory. But it's also bollocks.

Let's look at it for a second, shall we.

Advocates of digital or web psychology, and 'neuro-marketing' talk about things like Maslow's hierarchy of needs – safety, shelter, love, friendship all the way up to self-actualisation – and how you can help your customers achieve this stuff online. They talk about colour psychology – how the colour red supposedly increases arousal or heart rate, or how the colour blue apparently calms and evokes trust. How certain language or visuals are more likely to provoke an emotional response, or how certain titles will get more clicks than others because when we read it, it does something in this or that part of the brain.

All sounds very fucking cool, right? But the issue I have here is, psychologists i.e. people who have studied this for years and are qual'd up to their eyeballs, still know very little about how the mind works.

In the grand scheme of things, neuroscientists still don't really know much about how the nervous system affects how we act and think. A lot of it is still based on theory and guesswork.

So how the fuck can content marketers possibly know?

Do you realise how complicated those subjects are? Do you realise how little scientists actually know about what's going on in our heads?

When so little is known, how can we possibly expect marketers to use psychology and neuroscience effectively in marketing.

Do you see how dumb that sounds?

Until scientists themselves know more, in my opinion, people plugging these subjects when it comes to content creation are massively overcomplicating things.

And you know what? I'd hazard a guess that most marketers that sit there overanalysing this stuff probably aren't the ones producing the best content.

So, for now, let's keep it simple.

17. FUCK GRAMMAR

Oh, a writer said, "Fuck grammar." How edgy.

Right, so if you've ever read any of my stuff before, you'll know how important I think it is to keep things simple.

I mean, other than taking risks, this should be your top priority when it comes to creating content.

And I don't really mean 'fuck grammar'. But it's not as important as you might think, especially when it comes to social media.

Now before you spit your coffee out and start ranting about how I'm a twat on Twitter, let me make an argument.

If you look around, there are millions and millions of 'technically good' copywriters. But very few GOOD copywriters. There are millions of 'technically good' content creators. But very few GOOD content creators.

And what I mean by this is, tons of people know how to write well. They have good grammar, a real grasp of language, and, on the face of it, their writing appears top notch. But it gets no engagement. Nobody reads it. Nobody gives a shit about what they write.

But they continue to write the same way, because it's how they've been taught, their friends tell them its good, and their mum spends time at dinner parties talking about how their son or daughter is an 'amazing writer'.

You see, the vast majority of creatives, don't understand that content has one purpose and one purpose alone. To create an audience and, more often than not, eventually make money.

But if you're only getting 2 likes and a comment from your dad saying 'Great article, kid', I don't give a shit how 'technically good' your writing is, (and these words are gonna hurt) you, my friend, for the moment, are not a good writer. At least when it comes to marketing.

And here's another thing I can't get my head around. If that's the case, and you're a content producer who gets no engagement, and drives nothing to the business, why aren't you questioning that? Why aren't you looking in the mirror and going, "What I'm doing is shit. What can I do about it?"

Good writing (or design, or videography, or anything else creative) isn't about getting things perfect technically. When it comes to marketing, the only thing it's about is the end result.

So I'm going to say something controversial here. If you write an article and the grammar is perfect, and one of your colleagues writes an article and the grammar is shocking, but their article drives 10x more traffic and engagement than yours does, from a marketing perspective, theirs was the better piece of writing.

Hard to hear that, isn't it?

The fact is, creatives that are technically good are in the millions. Seriously, there are shitloads of writers, designers, videographers, illustrators etc. that are great at producing what can be considered technically good work. But creatives that can use their content to grow an audience, or bring in something tangible to the business – they're like gold dust.

Here's a tip that some writers won't like, either.

When it comes to social, when it comes to online content, when it comes to engaging a mass audience, please get good at one thing: writing the same way that you speak.

Now for most writers, this is painful. Academia fucked us.

We were all taught from a young age to write properly. Not to say 'me and Donald Trump' but to say 'Donald Trump and I', not to start sentences with 'And or But' and most of all, to make well-rounded arguments.

I'd like to say things have changed, but they haven't. Readers have always liked stuff that's easy to digest. The mass market doesn't really like jargon or the overuse of big words that they don't understand. So write for them. Don't write to show how many fancy words you know. The mass market doesn't read academic white papers, even in B2B. To be a good copywriter or content marketer, you need to take all of that writing shit that school, college and university taught you, chuck it out of the window, and learn to write again.

And as for making a well-rounded argument, don't. If you argue both sides of the thing you're writing about, it'll bring less people to the table. Why? Because people want to say their piece on the topic, and if you make their argument for them, they'll have less to say, and they won't comment on your post, or article. Your only job as a content producer is to light the fire - to spark the debate. It can be hard to leave parts of the argument out. It can be difficult to sit firmly on one side of the fence, knowing that you have more to say on a subject, but what you don't say is just as important as what you do when it comes to content marketing.

Now, most literary critics would look at my writing and say it's shit. I break all the rules I was told not to. To them I say, "Fuck your rules." I've hit over 10 million views on my content in the past 9 months, had just shy of 10,000 eBook downloads and got big results for tons of clients. Not only that, but my business, up until this point, has been built solely on inbound leads as a result of my own content. That's a brag, but it's also proof that what I say works.

However, I'm now going to contradict that last line with the next section.

18. FUCK WHAT I JUST SAID

Just because what I say works, doesn't mean that it works.

"What in the holy motherfucking fuck are you on about, Dan? If what you say might not work, why the hell am I reading this book?"

I know. I contradict myself a lot. I say some confusing stuff. I'm like one of those parents that smoke crack in front of their kids but tell them not to eat too many crisps because 'they're bad for you'. It's important to say at this stage, that I actually have no scientific proof that crack is worse for you than Quavers.

Anyway, what I'm trying to say is, the way that I write content will work for some of you. But, for most of you, if you follow what I say to the letter, it will bomb. Why? Because you're not me.

Most of you won't be able to get away with saying stuff like, "Your marketing team is as useless as a chocolate dildo." Most of you will look very 'try hard' if you start littering your copy with swearwords. And, let's be honest, most of you probably aren't funny either.

But what I can promise you is that, no matter what brand or sector I've produced content for, the following things are consistent.

People want to be spoken to like people. I don't care if you're B2C or B2B, lose the corporate bollocks. Bin the jargon. Stop with the shit acronyms.

The structure of good content has always remained the same. The hook (the title or first line of a piece of content) has to draw readers in. The body has to give them value and be relatable, and the close has to encourage them to act – whether that means a comment, a website visit or even a purchase.

Honesty is everything. If you're a brand, talk about your struggles as much as your successes. Admit it when you fuck up (see the 'FCK' KFC advert for a good example of this). Use the differing views of those within your organisation to show that you're not all corporate robots. Stop with the 'Our employees all have to sound the same' nonsense.

You need to test content repeatedly. Test messages. Experiment with different tones of voice. Not just at the start, but FOREVER. There is no blueprint to what works when it comes to marketing, nor will something that works necessarily continue to work. Those who fail at marketing are the ones that stick to what they've always known, are scared of taking risks, and never analyse what's going well and what's not.

Not all channels will work. If your business doesn't sell shit that's aesthetically pleasing or you don't have loads of good looking staff, you probably won't do very well on Instagram. If you're not the sort of brand that can have casual conversations with customers and take the piss out of competitors, Twitter is pretty pointless.

Unless you've got a solid budget, your Facebook campaigns will probably dive. If you're a boring accountant (sorry accountants) with the charisma of a dead slug, you'll most likely struggle to build a decent following on LinkedIn. Find one channel that works and, once you've mastered it, transfer that audience to other channels if you feel like you need them, and if you've got the time to manage them.

Aaannnndddd, back to the point about not listening to me. If you're truly creative, and if you try new types of content regularly, you will soon find your own way of doing things. You'll find things that work for you and wouldn't work for me or anyone else, and you might even find that things that I told you not to do, actually work for you.

If that's the case, what's the point of this book?

Well, I wrote this to give you things to think about. I know how difficult creating good content is, and I know how hard it can be to grow, and keep, an audience. But I also know that there is absolutely no blueprint for getting it right. None. You can read as many books like this one as you want. You can study as many great content creators as you want. You can get as many marketing quals, and learn as much about marketing psychology as you want. But nothing will ever replace good ol' trial and error. Nothing will ever replace 'learning on the job'.

Want to create fucking good content? Start by just creating content.

With a bit of talent and hard graft, you might just stumble upon something that works.

19. FUCKING GOOD CONTENT

To start, see if you can answer this. Below are 2 campaigns: Protein World and Nike. Both are examples of messages that were as controversial as they were successful. But what's the major difference between the approaches to these adverts?

Nike & Colin Kaepernick. The sportswear giant's market value rose by $6 billion after backing the former NFL quarterback.

Protein World. The brand made around £1 million in 4 days after this controversial campaign.

You know what I think the major difference is here?

Luck.

You see, Nike are known for their controversial marketing campaigns. They're known for firmly taking a stand.

The Colin Kaepernick ads were no different. It infuriated part of their audience to the extent that people actually bought items of Nike clothing and burnt them in the street.

On the surface, the Protein World campaign was equally controversial. It drove feminist groups and many others to deface the ads that were plastered across the London Underground.

Despite the controversy, both adverts drove profits.

But did Protein World ever manage to replicate the success of this campaign? Nope. And yet Nike continue to churn out successful campaign after successful campaign.

See the difference yet?

The fact is, I don't think Protein World realised what they'd done well. I think the campaign's success (and it was very successful, regardless of whether you or I agree with the message) was an accident.

And the fact that we've never seen any similar campaigns from them since, tells me that they haven't got a clue what they did to cause such a stir, or how to replicate it with further marketing.

Content marketing is about being like Nike. Not Protein World. It's about being able to create consistently good content.

Not a one off viral piece, or single successful campaign.

So what does good content do? What does it look like? How do you produce it?

Firstly, good content never sits on the fence. Ever. People, and small brands, are so scared of polarising opinion. But why?

Did Nike sit on the fence with Colin Kaepernick? Nope. Did it damage their brand? Nope.

Did Protein World worry about putting skinny models on advertisements on the underground with the caption, "Are you beach body ready?", and apologise when feminists lost their shit about it? Did they fuck.

In both cases, profits shot through the roof. I'm not saying I agree with Protein World's message, in fact I massively don't, but it spoke to their target demographic, and because of those that thought defacing posters with lipstick and girl power slogans would make a difference, the brand ended up all over the national news. Prime time TV slots and not a penny paid for it.

So, who came off better in the end?

And do you honestly think that Protein World gave a shit what I and so many other people who disagreed with their advert thought? Do you think that Nike cared that old, white blokes and racists were burning their trainers in response to the brand's support for Kaepernick?

The fact is, good content gets results. It says something powerful that strikes a chord with your target market. It has personality. It doesn't force products or services down people's throats. It's engaging.

And it always says something that your target market wish they could say, but daren't say.

We have a myriad of channels available to us to distribute content to the right people. Everyone has the tools at their finger tips to drive more traffic to their business.

Good content can't make up for a shit product. But one thing is certain. Good content will always work, no matter the social channel, no matter the advertising method, no matter the market.

If you get your content right, if you get your message nailed, if you find a tone of voice that makes you stand out, everything else will fall into place. But be very aware that it's only getting harder to do that.

You have to realise that we are currently experiencing content overload, and there is only so much our tiny minds can take in.

We walk down the street and we're bombarded with billboards, posters and company visuals. We watch telly or Youtube and we're subjected to boat loads of cringe-inducing ads and product placements. We scroll through social media feeds peppered with "Please buy our product" posts.

Just take a minute to think about how much content you see on a daily basis. Take a minute to imagine how difficult it is for new brands, products and services to stand out in that constant blitz of shite. Take a minute to think how absolutely fucking pointless your boring corporate blog is.

And if you don't start doing something about it now, I'm afraid to say that things will only get worse.

20. A FUCKING GOOD VOICE

When it comes to tone of voice, you know what I've found works consistently?

Authenticity. Urgh. That word again.

Now, I know you're probably rolling your eyes right now. Every marketing knobhead and their dog harps on about creating authentic content. What they don't tend to be good at is explaining what 'authentic' means.

You've probably tried to create authentic content. And it's probably bombed. That's why you bought this book, I'm guessing. You tried to put some personality into your copy, or images, or videos and nobody gave a fuck, so you stopped trying and went back to the corporate garbage you were producing before. And, honestly, I get it. It's disheartening. It takes a lot of effort to produce material and when it achieves very little, it feels like a massive waste of time. Which, I won't lie to you, it is.

Getting your tone of voice right isn't easy. If it were, we'd all be amazing writers, designers and videographers, and we'd be swimming in so much incredible content that incredible content wouldn't be incredible anymore. It takes time.

Now, when I talk about content, and tone of voice, I'm talking about it with marketing your brand in mind. I'm not talking about content for white papers, or academic courses, or law text books. That's not my gig, and never will be. This is about producing content, and a tone of voice, that helps you to sell more products, or services or whatever.

And do you know how you do that?

Firstly, be human. Talk like a fucking person. Bin off the initialisms, acronyms and jargon.

Secondly, keep it simple. It doesn't matter what industry you're in, using big words and unnecessary language will just alienate people and will do nothing for you other than ensure you come across as a bit of a wanker.

Thirdly, never underestimate the power of humour. In any market. And I mean any market.

Your tone of voice is what you'll become known for. People might not necessarily remember everything that you write, but they will remember they way you write and how it makes them feel. And what I've found is, in some industries, particularly the corporate ones where nobody really produces any stand out content, making an impact can be as simple as changing your tone of voice.

Like I said, you need to take risks, but for many of you, small changes will make a big impact.

21. A FUCKING GOOD HOOK

Every single piece of online content needs a hook. Period.

Let me repeat that for those at the back, with an F-bomb added in for impact.

EVERY. PIECE. OF. CONTENT. NEEDS. A. FUCKING. HOOK.

What's a hook? It's the first line, or title of content that is written in such a way that it draws readers, or viewers, in.

Call it clickbait, call it a hook, call it sensationalist bullshit, call it whatever you want. It's the only way you'll build an audience quickly. Especially at first.

You see, I think clickbait and hooks are different. Not in the way they're written, but in the content that they lead to. If you write something controversial, or sensationalist, and it doesn't lead to something of value to your audience, that's clickbait. If it does lead to something valuable, in my eyes, that's a hook.

And don't assume value is just new information, or insights or whatever, as most people do. Value comes in many forms. Making them laugh, making them cry, giving them stories that they can relate to and not feel alone in their thoughts - they're all things that are valuable to your audience.

Like I always say, content marketing is supposed to drive sales. And when do people buy?

When they feel good. Or they buy to avoid pain, which, in turn, makes them feel good. They buy when they feel connected, or part of something. And they buy when other people do, because when a product, service or brand is trusted by loads of their peers, they're more likely to trust it too. We all suffer from herd mentality. That's why I harp on so much about not fucking selling. You shouldn't have to sell. If you make a connection with your audience, they'll buy when they're ready. You've already done the hard part by getting them to buy into you.

A hook is a massive part of that. If you don't draw your readers in, it doesn't matter how much value your content contains, it'll be a waste of time, because no-one will bother reading it. And if nobody reads it, nobody buys, do they?

On social media especially, you have a very small window to capture someone's attention. We're talking milliseconds. And if your title, or the first couple of lines aren't engaging enough, they've already scrolled past.

And, as your audience grows bigger and bigger, hooks become less important. I'm not saying you should revert back to shit titles and boring first lines, but once people know you for good content, your name above a post will be enough to draw them in.

"Right, so I just write some controversial shit to try and get my audience to click then?"

Not necessarily. Don't underestimate how difficult it can be to write a good hook. If you've ever tried to think up a good title for an article, you'll know already how hard it is.

Here are a few things you can try to help you come up with that killer first line or title:

- Write the piece first, then take the most polarising element of the post or article, and fashion that into a short, impactful hook.

- If the topic of your content is controversial, funny, topical, or downright weird, just keep it simple and say it how it is.

- Use a twist. So, in the first line or title, say the complete opposite. Is the article about how important maternity pay is? Say that you don't agree with it, then flip it around in the piece itself.

If you do what I say, and test content and keep track of what works, you'll come up with your own ways of writing hooks. And the more you write them, and the more you analyse what drove the most traffic, the more you'll become familiar with what works.

We've already talked about the amount of content we're all subjected to on a daily basis.

And that's because SEO isn't what it once was, PPC costs a fucking wedge, social advertising is sketchy and tough to get right, and email's pretty much in the fucking bin for most companies that bought shit data or whatever. So now, everyone is trying content marketing. They're trying to drive business organically. They're desperate to go viral. They want to stand out.

The hook, my content-creating, little pals, is more important than ever. If you can't hook your audience in, your content that you worked so hard to create will just get lost in that sea of complete and utter, dry, rubbish, boring, corporate crap.

And we don't want that now, do we?

22. FUCKING GOOD CONTENT RULES

1. Stop trying to produce content on every social media platform. If you sell false teeth, your target demographic probably aren't on Insta, are they? Nobody wants to look at pictures of gummy old people dribbling soup onto their cardigans. Find out where your customers are and get really fucking good at one or two channels. For most B2B stuff, LinkedIn's your man.

2. As wanky as this is going to sound, think outside the box. And, what I mean by that is, ask yourself, "what are my competitors doing to market themselves?" and then DON'T DO THAT. I don't care how well it works for them. If you do the same thing, as a lot of companies seem to think they have to do, one of two things will happen. Either, you'll produce marketing that looks like a poor man's version of the stuff your competitor is doing, or you'll bring more of the same stuff to market which will bore your customers and ruin the party for everyone.

3. Start with simple changes. You don't have to ride a zebra through a hospital, shouting, "The NHS can wank my dad!" whilst naked and carrying a giant flag with your logo on, just to make people aware of your new healthcare software. In a lot of industries, content - and marketing efforts in general - are so ridiculously shit that even something simple like a different, casual tone of voice can make your content stand out.

4. Get your message and tone of voice right before you try anything else. You don't need to jump straight into videos, memes, ebooks and keynote speeches. Start with really simple content. Refine it until you get a decent amount of engagement, then analyse the shit out of it until you've figured out what works. Only once you know the sort of stuff your target audience react to should you start diversfying your content.

5. Stop wasting time writing million-page marketing strategies

before you've even tested your content on your market. Think up a load of ideas for content that won't take up a shed load of time and resources, push it out, analyse what worked, and then begin to build your strategy and campaigns around the topics that resonated with the people you're trying to reach.

6. Don't put money behind any content before knowing that your target audience want to see it. If you have an infographic that took you 5 hours to design but only got 3 likes because, in reality, it's shit, putting money behind it will only push it out to a wider audience, who will also think it's shit.

7. You probably don't have to produce as much content as 'experts' will have you believe. If you're a small business, or a business without a marketing team, you probably don't have time to produce daily content. Being creative is taxing. If marketing isn't your main job, you've only got limited time to come up with stuff. It's much smarter to produce one piece of decent content per week that gets a good amount of engagement from your target audience, than 2 posts a day that get less interest than a dick pic on Tinder.

8. Build an audience. Content marketing isn't a quick fix. In fact, no types of marketing are a quick fix. It takes time to build your audience, and it can take a while to start producing material that they actually want to see. But, if you take the time to capture an audience, you'll be able to sell anything to them. That's why, even though Kylie Jenner is the epitome of everything that's wrong with society, she could probably come out with a brand of fake eyelashes made from the pubic hair of homeless greek men, and her fans would snap them up.

9. You don't have to talk about subjects that relate to your product all the time. Your target market will have other interests.

#pubelashes

Maybe your ideal customers are accountants with their own practices. They're business owners too, so produce content that relates to them in that respect. You can even talk about hobbies, your company culture, hiring, or managing people. To build an audience, people want authentic content. Not just industry 'expertise'.

10. Don't buy the bullshit. In the cloudy world of marketing, full of shady agencies, tinpot qualifications, and 'influencers' with fake audiences, it can be easy to get drawn in by the bollocks. But don't listen to anyone that says something like, "[insert channel here] is dead." You see it all the time. Twitter's dead. And yet, there are millions of people still using it every day. Postal advertising is dead. And yet, people still have letter boxes. I used to be guilty of it. But, those who say things are dead, just haven't been creative enough. Imagine wrapping your leaflet around butt plugs and posting them through the letter boxes of potential customers. Are you honestly telling me that wouldn't get people talking? You can have that idea for free.

23. FUCK SUNSHINE & RAINBOWS

There are, as with anything, things that can go wrong with content. Especially when you make it personal and include the opinions and stories of those within your business.

Firstly, there are things that you might say that could damage both your company, and personal brand. You know the sort of things I mean. My rule has always been, your content should never really attack an individual. Take the piss out of stereotypes? Sure. Attack social norms? Go for it. Use celebs in weird analogies? Of course. But never get personal with people. Never be malicious. And never, ever fucking dream of discriminating.

But that's an obvious risk, right? We all know opinions can be dangerous. People may not take what you say as intended.

There are a few other less obvious risks though.

I always say three things. Be yourself, polarise opinion, and be honest.

But here's the issue. If you polarise opinion outside, there is a danger you'll polarise opinion inside your organisation too. The guys working for you will also see your content. There's a chance they won't agree with the things you say. Or, for that matter, the things your company says. That can cause problems.

It's also important that, if you're going to talk about your company on social media, especially when it comes to things like culture and management, you better be sure that you practice what you preach. Think about it for a second. Imagine writing an article on why it's a dickhead move to micromanage employees. On how getting the best out of your people means leaving them to do their job. But, in reality, you have the self-awareness of a brain damaged goldfish, and didn't realise that most of your team feel as though you stifle their work by breathing down their necks every 5 minutes. What do you think that will do to your working relationships when those who work for you think the content you're pushing out to the rest of the world is complete bollocks?

Do you see what I'm getting at? Transparency has to exist on both sides of the business. What you push out has to paint an honest picture of what actually goes on inside your organisation.

Otherwise, whilst your sales go from strength to strength, your internal culture will nosedive.

"So, Dan. Why end on a negative, you massive fun gobbler?"

Because that's reality.

You don't have to always end on a high note. You don't have to be positive, for the sake of being positive.

There are risks to this, like anything else. But if you don't take those risks, your content will remain vanilla.

Dry.

Boring as fuck.

And if you sit on the fence all the time, no one will give a shit about you. They'll become indifferent to your brand.

So be bold. Be daring. Try stuff that no one else has. Be weirder than a bat's vagina.

After all, it's our differences that make us stand out.

And so I leave you with something that was said at the 'Take Fucking Risks' event in London.

This isn't word for word, as I'd had a few beers, but here goes.

"If you always act based on knowledge, you'll never do anything different."

How fucking true is that?

24. FUCK THIS, I'M OUTTA HERE

Well, there you have it. My thoughts on content.

Sure I probably need to wash my mouth out with soap, and yes, there is a possibility I'm edging closer and closer to career suicide with every weird piece of content I create, but hopefully you got something from this. Hopefully, in amongst the profanity, sexual references and bizarre analogies you managed to find something valuable.

Because although I may not be everyone's cup of tea, a lot of what I say works. And, people, I cannot stress this enough; creating good content isn't rocket science. We all have it in us to build an audience. Admittedly, some of us a smaller audience that consists of our mum, our Grandma, the kid with the strange eye from school and an anonymous stalker, but still an audience.

Lastly, let me give you my final rule, which applies to both content creation and life.

Whether you're white, black, tall, short, fat, thin, skinny, hench, female, male, gender fluid, a model, uglier than Theresa May whilst eating a lemon, a sexually-diseased sheep fondler, straight, gay, bisexual, asexual, disabled, not disabled, mentally ill, not mentally ill (even though we're all mentally ill if you think about it), religious, atheist, an actual god, a foot fetishist, dyslexic, the best writer on the planet, a tory, a TV chef, a traffic warden, a creepy lifeguard, a vegan, a children's entertainer, a millionaire, on the dole, a house owner or homeless...don't be a dickhead.

If you think that a piece of content could paint you as a dickhead in any way, I'd advise you not to do it. And that's coming from me. Don't discriminate. Don't attack an underdog. And try not to attack an individual.

Go after concepts and ideals. Have opinions. Take a stand for those who need it and struggle to do so themselves. Say the things that most people are thinking.

It's stuff like that that will gain you admiration and respect. It's stuff like that that'll help you build an audience.

Good luck, content creators.

Printed in Great Britain
by Amazon